RUBIK'S QUEST

MISSION INVENT

JOHN FARNDON

QEB

QEB Publishing

Cover Design: Rosie Levine
Illustrators: David Shephard
and Lyndon White
Editor: Amanda Askew
Designer: Punch Bowl Design
QEB Project Editor: Ruth Symons
Editorial Director: Victoria Garrard
Art Director: Laura Roberts-Jensen

Picture credits (t=top, b=bottom, l=left, r=right, c=center)

shutterstock 28b 39b Designua, 47br AlexRoz; **Bigstock** 23b 29r 34 homestudio

First published in the US in 2014
by QEB Publishing, Inc.
3 Wrigley, Suite A, Irvine, CA 92618

www.qed-publishing.co.uk

A CIP record for this book is available from
the Library of Congress.

ISBN 978 1 60992 620 5

Printed in China

How to begin your adventure

Are you ready for an awesome adventure in which you must solve mind-bending puzzles? Then you've come to the right place!

Mission Invent isn't an ordinary book—you don't read the pages in order, 1, 2, 3. . . Instead you jump forward and backward through the book as you face a series of challenges. Sometimes you may lose your way, but the story will always guide you back to where you need to be.

The story begins on page 4. Straight away there are questions to answer and problems to overcome. The questions will look something like this:

IF YOU THINK THE CORRECT ANSWER IS A, GO TO PAGE 37

IF YOU THINK THE CORRECT ANSWER IS B, GO TO PAGE 11

Your task is to solve each problem. If you think the correct answer is A, turn to page 37 and look for the matching symbol in red. That's where you will find the next part of the story. If you make the wrong choice, the text will explain where you went wrong and let you have another chance.

The problems in this book are all about machines and engineering. To solve them, you must use your knowledge and common sense. To help you, there's a glossary of useful words at the back of the book, starting on page 44.

ARE YOU READY?
Turn the page and let your adventure begin!

MISSION INVENT

You love being an apprentice designer at Toy Towers, where they make the world's most amazing toys. You wish you could meet the owner, Mr. Jollypops.

You arrive one morning to find Mr. Jollypops's assistant waiting for you.

Mr. Jollypops wants to see you urgently. He will explain everything.

HOW INTRIGUING! WHAT COULD MR. JOLLYPOPS WANT WITH YOU? **FIND OUT** ON PAGE 12

No, clockwork mechanisms only got their name because they were first invented to drive the hands on clocks.

GO BACK TO PAGE 33
TO **TRY AGAIN**

No, a straight bar does not convert your pedaling power to turn the wheels.

GO BACK
TO PAGE 28

The next morning, the box is open and your camera is on the floor. There's a photo of some yellow shoes, but you don't recognize them.

Luckily, there's no damage to your car. You roll it out to the starting grid, where your rivals are already waiting.

START LINE

5.5 lb handicap

4.3 lb handicap

6.1 lb handicap

747.3 N

Every car in the race must weigh exactly the same, no matter how heavy the driver is. To do this, each driver is weighed, and then given a "handicap" weight. This takes them and their car up to the right weight.

The weighing machine shows your weight in NEWTONS, rather than pounds! Should you tell the steward that the weighing machine is faulty?

ABSOLUTELY
GO TO PAGE 42

NO, JUST GO WITH IT
HEAD OVER TO PAGE 24

Right answer! Gravity is the force that pulls the roller coaster carriage faster and faster as it runs down the slope. It has no need of an engine!

You open the door and step out into the street.

YOUNG TOYMAKER OF THE YEAR COMPETITION HERE TODAY!

Cranky Colin

Candy Clockwork

Rod Axle

Wow! What an event! You head to the garages. An announcement booms out from the loudspeakers.

The Young Toymaker of the Year competition involves three tasks to test the ability of our young contestants. The winner will be awarded $1 million!

CHALLENGE 1: BUILD A GO-KART

The fastest car in a straight-line race will win. Hurry to your workstations!

Spanner Spike

Mechanical Mavis

Toy Towers

YOU ALL **RUN TO YOUR WORKSTATIONS** ON PAGE 31

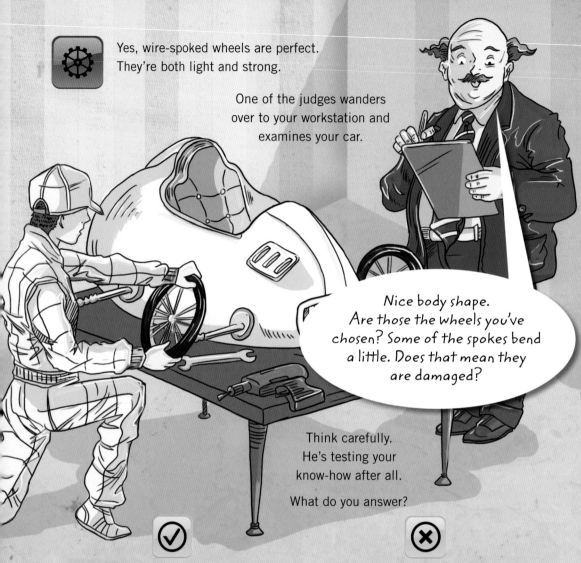

Yes, wire-spoked wheels are perfect. They're both light and strong.

One of the judges wanders over to your workstation and examines your car.

Nice body shape. Are those the wheels you've chosen? Some of the spokes bend a little. Does that mean they are damaged?

Think carefully. He's testing your know-how after all.

What do you answer?

YES, THEY MUST BE DAMAGED!
YOU NEED TO GET SOME NEW ONES QUICKLY.
HEAD OVER TO PAGE 27

NO, THE SPOKES ARE FINE.
THE FLEXIBILITY KEEPS THE WHEELS STABLE.
GO TO PAGE 33

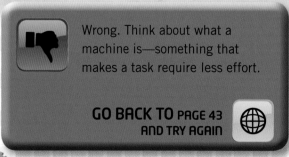

Wrong. Think about what a machine is—something that makes a task require less effort.

GO BACK TO PAGE 43 AND TRY AGAIN

No, you'd need to affix the pulley wheel to the ceiling first.

GO BACK TO PAGE 20

Oh my. The soldier may look small, but he's made of lead and weighs 200 pounds. As soon as you step in the basket and release the hook, you both plummet downward.

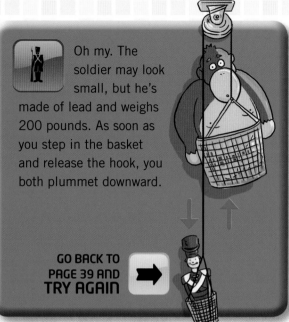

GO BACK TO PAGE 39 AND TRY AGAIN

 No, a gear and knob won't allow you to turn the mechanism inside the door.

GO BACK TO PAGE 30

 No, the effort is the force that you apply to a machine to make something happen.

RETURN TO PAGE 42

That's right! Just as you finish tightening the last nut, a stranger in overalls strolls over, checks no one is listening, then whispers:

Do you want a can of oil to rub on your tires to make you go faster?

Apart from the fact that it would be cheating, would it help you? What do you say?

GREAT, THE OIL WILL REDUCE THE FRICTION—
YOU'LL BE THE FASTEST OUT THERE!
GO TO PAGE 16

NO, OIL WILL JUST MAKE THINGS HARDER.
GO AWAY!
TURN TO PAGE 28

No, pushing the lever forward will only open the trapdoor further.

GO BACK TO PAGE 19 AND **TRY AGAIN**

No, an inflated balloon could drift away and the cheater could easily escape.

BACK TO PAGE 13 TO **TRY AGAIN**

Correct! By adding the rack and pinion, the steering mechanism works perfectly.

You line up at the starting point, ready for the next race.

PINION

RACK

START! You power along, moving from last to fourth. Cranky Colin crashes on the first bend because his steering fails. Candy Clockwork spins off the track too, because she takes the second bend too fast.

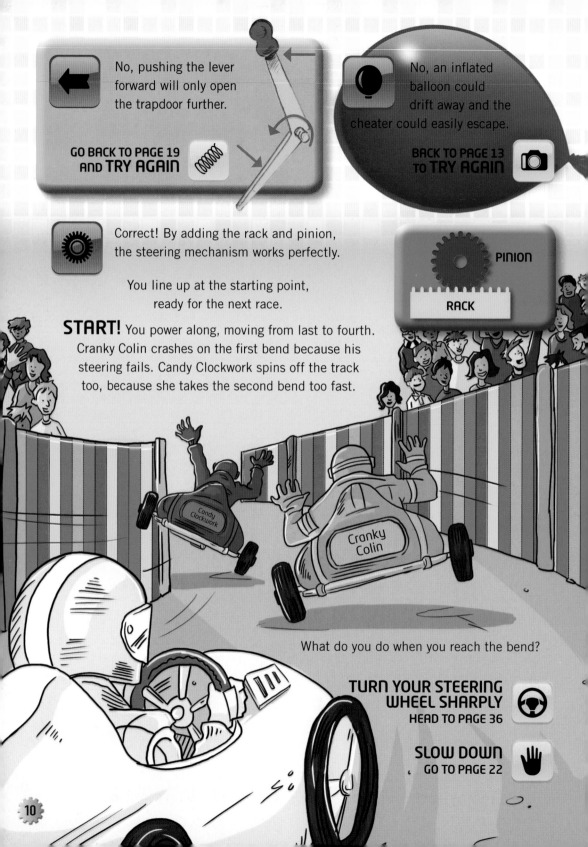

What do you do when you reach the bend?

TURN YOUR STEERING WHEEL SHARPLY
HEAD TO PAGE 36

SLOW DOWN
GO TO PAGE 22

Yes, a piston provides the strong pushing force. You whiz up the tower!

A crackly voice comes from a speaker in the elevator.

This is Mr. Jollypops. I have something important to tell you—but only if you can pass the tests and reach my office. Good luck!

When the doors open at the top, your way is blocked by a mechanical knight. There's a switch on its chest, with two positions, and a small plaque.

TO DISENGAGE THIS MACHINE, WHAT IS AN AUTOMATON?

Which position do you push the lever to?

A REMOTE-CONTROLLED MACHINE. GO TO PAGE 27

A SELF-OPERATING MACHINE. FLIP TO PAGE 33

Mr. Jollypops's office is at the top of the highest tower, so you need to take the superfast elevator. There's a bright red sign on the elevator door.

TO OPEN THE DOORS, ANSWER THIS QUESTION: IS THIS ELEVATOR HYDRAULIC OR PNEUMATIC? PRESS THE CORRECT BUTTON.
Clue: The elevator uses fluid to move

HYDRAULIC

 TURN TO PAGE 21

PNEUMATIC

 HEAD OVER TO PAGE 37

 No, in a suspension bridge, the bridge is suspended from looping cables hung between towers. You don't have cables or anything to hang them from.

GO BACK TO PAGE 32

 CHALLENGE 2: ORAL EXAM

You are each taken into a room to answer questions in front of a panel of judges.

Question one: Which Greek scientist came up with the theory of levers more than 2,000 years ago?

 ARCIMBOLDO
GO TO PAGE 20

 ARCHAEOPTERYX
HEAD TO PAGE 33

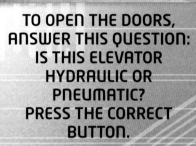 **ARCHIMEDES**
FLIP TO PAGE 43

Great, a camera will do the trick!

You have a few leftover parts on your workstation. If you're smart, you can fix the camera so it will pop up and take a picture the moment anyone opens the box.

Which part should you use to affix the camera to the box?

BALLOON
GO TO PAGE 10

RUBBER BAND
TURN TO PAGE 19

COIL SPRING
FLIP TO PAGE 36

All of these are important elements of more complex machines, but they aren't simple machines.

GO BACK TO PAGE 23 AND **TRY AGAIN**

No, electricity is a force, but it plays no part in the movement of a roller coaster. Roller coasters are driven by gravity and momentum alone.

CHOOSE AGAIN ON PAGE 41

No, you've spelled out motion, which is the power of movement.

GO BACK TO PAGE 29 AND **TRY AGAIN**

Yes, the gorilla may be big, but he's very light at only 10 pounds. You release the hook, and zoom straight to the top as the soldier plummets downward. You've made it to Mr. Jollypops's office!

Mr. Jollypops turns to look at you.

You've done well to pass my tests! I've called you here because Toy Towers is in danger of closing. Everything is riding on the Young Toymaker of the Year competition and its $1 million prize. I've trained a junior designer for this competition, but she's sick. I want you to take her place.

I'd love to. I won't let you down!

I have little time to teach you. Toys may look shiny and wonderful, but it's important to know what's on their insides. For example, what is the mechanism inside a Rubik's Cube?

RUBBER BANDS
GO TO PAGE 18

WHEELS AND AXLES
TURN TO PAGE 36

A SPRING
FLIP TO PAGE 23

No, wood is far too heavy for a go-kart! You'd need a horse to pull it!

BACK TO PAGE 26 TO **TRY AGAIN**

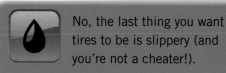 No, the last thing you want tires to be is slippery (and you're not a cheater!).

TRY AGAIN ON PAGE 9

 As you're tightening the wheel nuts and knocking out the dents from your crash, a judge enters your garage.

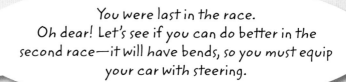 You were last in the race. Oh dear! Let's see if you can do better in the second race—it will have bends, so you must equip your car with steering.

The judge hands you a steering wheel.

You'll need to link the steering wheel to a rod, which connects to the car's front wheels. As you turn the wheel, the rod will move from side to side to swivel the wheels. What type of gear do you need to connect the wheel to the rod?

Which gear do you ask for?

 WORM GEAR
TURN TO PAGE 28

 SPUR GEAR
GO TO PAGE 39

 RACK AND PINION
HEAD OVER TO PAGE 10

Yes, turning the handle turns a series of cams. A cam is a wheel with a bump. As each cam turns, its bump pushes up a segment of the caterpillar.

CAM WHEELS

Correct! I'm confident that you'll be a great contender in the competition. You must hurry though—it starts in under an hour. Here's a shortcut...

Mr. Jollypops opens a door straight onto a roller coaster carriage! You sit inside it behind a lever to release the brakes.

To go forward, choose the lever named after the effectiveness of a machine.

ROBOT BOOST

MECHANICAL ADVANTAGE

AUTOMATIC EFFECT

Which do you choose?

THE MECHANICAL ADVANTAGE
TURN TO PAGE 41

THE ROBOT BOOST
HEAD OVER TO PAGE 21

THE AUTOMATIC EFFECT
FLIP TO PAGE 30

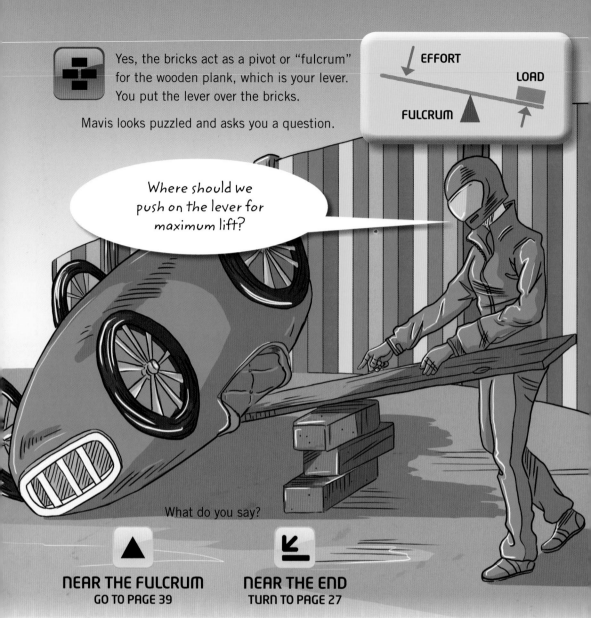

Yes, the bricks act as a pivot or "fulcrum" for the wooden plank, which is your lever. You put the lever over the bricks.

Mavis looks puzzled and asks you a question.

Where should we push on the lever for maximum lift?

EFFORT

LOAD

FULCRUM

What do you say?

NEAR THE FULCRUM
GO TO PAGE 39

NEAR THE END
TURN TO PAGE 27

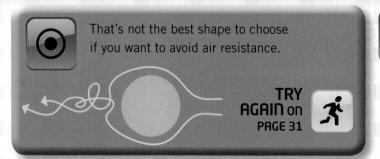

That's not the best shape to choose if you want to avoid air resistance.

TRY AGAIN on
PAGE 31

No, there are no rubber bands in a Rubik's Cube.

SPRING BACK TO PAGE 14 AND TRY AGAIN

Not this time! A screw is turned, like a door handle, but it keeps going around rather than just back and forth.

HAVE ANOTHER TRY
ON PAGE 30

 The camera would simply hang on a rubber band, so the cheater could easily be missed.

TRY AGAIN ON PAGE 13

 Yes, the power comes from a coiled metal spring. You put the spring into the toy and wind the key to tighten it. As the spring unwinds, it drives the mechanism and the toy comes to life. It moves forward, pushing the key straight into the lock.

You open the door, but there's an open trapdoor on the other side. There's no way around it. A large iron bar controls the trapdoor.

Which way do you move the bar to shut the trapdoor?

FORWARD
TURN TO PAGE 10

BACKWARD
GO TO PAGE 39

Correct! The load is the weight that is moved by a simple machine, such as a pile of bricks lifted by a crane.

You run through the left-hand doorway. You need to hurry before the cheating Spanner Spike or any of the others catch up with you.

You reach a dead end. On the wall is an image of a stairway with missing stairs.

Which simple machine would you use to cross the gap?

A WEDGE
TURN TO PAGE 38

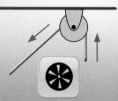

A PULLEY
GO TO PAGE 8

An INCLINED PLANE
FLIP TO PAGE 29

 Cabbage head! Arcimboldo was an Italian artist who painted pictures of heads made from vegetables.

GO BACK
TO PAGE 12

 Well done! The kinks are called cranks. Cranks turn the up-and-down motion of your pedaling legs into the round-and-round motion you need to turn the wheels.

PULL ON BRAKE CABLE

You read the final—and very important—instruction.

What do you add to pull on the brake cable?

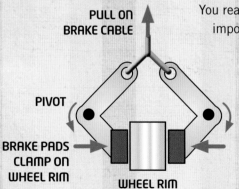

PIVOT

BRAKE PADS CLAMP ON WHEEL RIM

WHEEL RIM

Step 4
Add brakes.

A TOGGLE
GO TO PAGE 31

A LEVER
TURN TO PAGE 37

An electric shock may startle the wrong-doer, but you still won't know who it is.

 Wrong! That's just made up!

GO BACK TO PAGE 37
TO TRY AGAIN

GO BACK TO PAGE 17
AND CHOOSE AGAIN

 Incorrect! Think about how you use a wheelbarrow—it has handles to lever up the body, and then a wheel to move it along.

TRY AGAIN
ON PAGE 40 AB

 You've got it! A hydraulic system uses pressurized liquid to move a machine's parts.

As you enter the elevator, you see two buttons and a question.

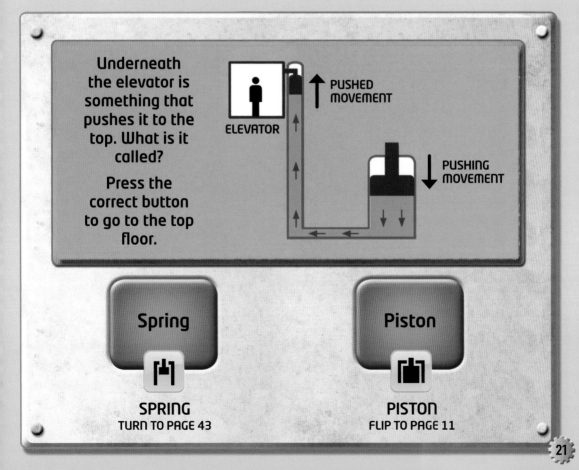

Underneath the elevator is something that pushes it to the top. What is it called?

Press the correct button to go to the top floor.

ELEVATOR

PUSHED MOVEMENT

PUSHING MOVEMENT

Spring

Piston

SPRING
TURN TO PAGE 43

PISTON
FLIP TO PAGE 11

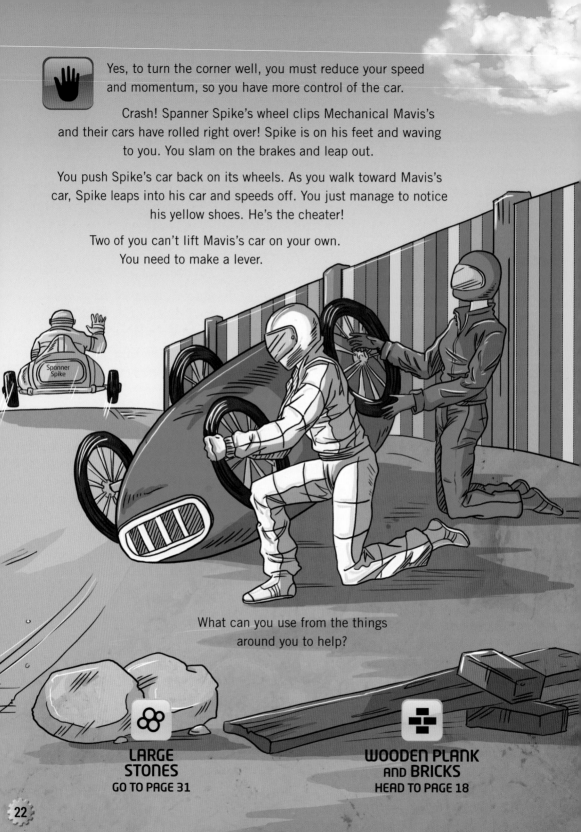

Yes, to turn the corner well, you must reduce your speed and momentum, so you have more control of the car.

Crash! Spanner Spike's wheel clips Mechanical Mavis's and their cars have rolled right over! Spike is on his feet and waving to you. You slam on the brakes and leap out.

You push Spike's car back on its wheels. As you walk toward Mavis's car, Spike leaps into his car and speeds off. You just manage to notice his yellow shoes. He's the cheater!

Two of you can't lift Mavis's car on your own. You need to make a lever.

What can you use from the things around you to help?

LARGE STONES
GO TO PAGE 31

WOODEN PLANK AND BRICKS
HEAD TO PAGE 18

Correct! In fact, it's two machines. The handle is a lever that allows you to apply more force. The blade is a wedge—a triangular shape that concentrates effort along a thin, pointed edge.

Final, killer question: What are the six simple machines from which all others are built?

THE LEVER, WHEEL AND AXLE, PULLEY, WEDGE, RAMP, AND SCREW.
HEAD TO PAGE 30

THE CAM, CRANK, GEAR, BOW, BALL-BEARING, AND DRILL.
GO TO PAGE 13

THE CRANK, LEVER, HAMMER, WHEEL AND AXLE, PLOUGH, AND SCREW.
TURN TO PAGE 42

 No, a Rubik's Cube doesn't contain a spring.

GO BACK TO PAGE 14 AND TRY AGAIN

 No, turning the nut counterclockwise loosens it.

GO BACK TO PAGE 33 AND TRY AGAIN

Correct! You've spelled out momentum. The momentum of an object can only be changed if another force acts upon it. For example, a ball rolling down a hill has momentum. It will only stop if an object blocks its way.

You carefully step on the correct squares—but Spanner Spike is running up behind you, following your steps. He's cheating again! You both lunge for the Cube, but Spanner Spike gets there first. As soon as he touches it, light floods down and you are both lifted up into another room.

GO TO THE AWARD CEREMONY ON PAGE 43

Correct! Newtons are the measurement for weight, which is actually the force of gravity pulling on an object.

You're each given your handicaps and are ready to start.

THREE! TWO! ONE! GO!

You all lurch forward on the straight track. Spanner Spike takes the lead, but a bump in the road slows him down. Rod Axle moves up to pole position.

Spanner Spike gains on Rod Axle and then bumps him off the course. As you pull alongside Spanner Spike, he bumps you down the slope too!

Toy Towers

Your car is ok, but it's a steep hill to pedal back up. How are you going to get the extra power to climb the slope?

SELECT A LOW GEAR
TURN TO PAGE 41

SELECT A HIGH GEAR
GO TO PAGE 38

Yes, a teardrop is the perfect shape for air to slip smoothly by on either side.

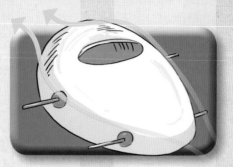

You read the next instruction.

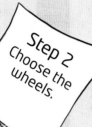
Step 2
Choose the wheels.

Now, this is tricky. You need to add wheels that are light, but strong so they don't become damaged during the race.

What do you go for?

WIRE-SPOKED WHEELS
GO TO PAGE 8

SOLID ALUMINUM WHEELS
HEAD TO PAGE 30

WOODEN-SPOKED WHEELS
FLIP TO PAGE 16

 No, the planks will slip apart in the middle because nothing is holding them securely enough.

GO BACK TO PAGE 38

 No! If it needed a battery, it would be called a battery toy!

 Oh dear, there may be screws in a crane, but that's not the key part!

GO BACK TO PAGE 33 AND **TRY AGAIN**

GO BACK TO PAGE 43 AND **ANSWER QUICKLY**

No, an automaton isn't operated by remote control.

TRY AGAIN ON PAGE 11

 No, superglue won't help at all!

 SUPERGLUE

HAVE ANOTHER TRY ON PAGE 37

 Get a grip! This is how they're meant to be. If the spokes are too stiff, the wheels will keep on bouncing off little bumps in the track.

FLEXIBLE = LESS BOUNCE

RIGID = MORE BOUNCE

HAVE ANOTHER TRY ON PAGE 8

It works! You both push down on one end of the lever, which lifts the car at the other end. Soon Mavis's car is back on its wheels.

By now, Spanner Spike is almost at the finish line. As he looks back at you, he skids off the track into the judges' table!

You and Mavis are still laughing as you approach the finish line together. You tie for first.

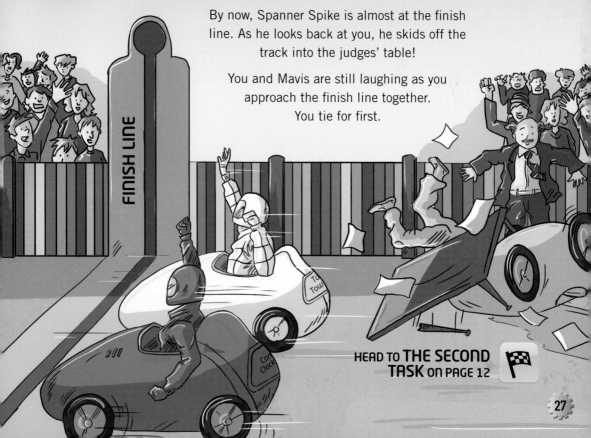

FINISH LINE

HEAD TO **THE SECOND TASK** ON PAGE 12

No! Gears are pairs of wheels with interlocking teeth. They are used for many things, but they aren't used in a wriggling caterpillar.

GO BACK TO PAGE 36 AND TRY AGAIN

Correct! Tires are made of rubber to be extra sticky, so they grip the road for good acceleration, braking, and cornering. This is called traction.

You get back to reading the instructions. A bell just rang meaning that you've got only ten minutes left.

There are two pedal bars provided.
Which do you choose?

Step 3
Add
pedals.

**THE
STRAIGHT BAR**
GO TO PAGE 5

**THE BAR
WITH KINKS**
HEAD OVER TO PAGE 20

No, a worm gives a powerful turning motion, like a screw, but not the side-to-side movement you need for steering.

**HAVE ANOTHER
TRY ON PAGE 16**

Excellent! An inclined plane is a ramp that would help you to get across the gap. The wall lifts up to reveal a room. At one end is the Golden Cube. The instructions say:

TO GET ACROSS, SPELL THE MISSING WORD BY STEPPING ON ONLY THE CORRECT SQUARES. A MOVING OBJECT IS PROPELLED FORWARD BY ITS MASS. THIS IS CALLED...............

In which order do you step across the colored squares?

PATH A:
GREEN, BLUE, RED, YELLOW, BLUE, ORANGE, YELLOW, BLUE.
GO TO PAGE 23

PATH B:
GREEN, BLUE, ORANGE, RED, ORANGE, YELLOW.
HEAD TO PAGE 13

PATH C:
GREEN, YELLOW, BLUE, GREEN, YELLOW, GREEN, BLUE, GREEN, ORANGE.
FLIP TO PAGE 36

Correct! The lever, wheel and axle, pulley, wedge, ramp, and screw are all simple machines.

The judge stares at you with a blank expression, before breaking into a smile.

"Three out of three, great! Now for TASK 3: The Golden Cube maze. Reach the Golden Cube first to claim the $1 million prize."

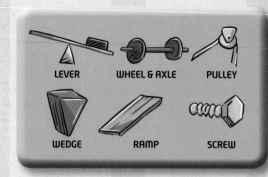

LEVER WHEEL & AXLE PULLEY

WEDGE RAMP SCREW

She points toward a door. You take a deep breath and head toward it. There isn't a handle!

TO MAKE A HANDLE, USE THE PIECES IN THIS BOX.

A. KNOB

B. ROD

C. GEAR

D. SCREW

Which objects do you use to make a handle?

AB
KNOB AND ROD
GO TO PAGE 40

AC
KNOB AND GEAR
HEAD TO PAGE 9

AD
KNOB AND SCREW
FLIP TO PAGE 19

That's not right! There's no such thing as "the automatic effect."

HAVE ANOTHER TRY ON PAGE 17

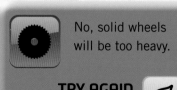

No, solid wheels will be too heavy.

TRY AGAIN ON PAGE 26

Although you could place stones under the car to hold it up, you'd need to be able to lift it first.

GO BACK
TO PAGE 22

No, when you pull on a toggle, it doesn't give your muscles any extra pulling power. So the brakes will be weak.

HEAD BACK
TO PAGE 20

There's a set of instructions on the bench, but they're not very detailed!

*Step 1
Choose the body shell.*

You know that you should choose a body shell that allows the air to slip by more easily as you hurtle through it.

Which shape will work best?

CUBE
GO TO
PAGE 41

TEARDROP
TURN TO PAGE 26

SPHERE
HEAD TO
PAGE 18

Correct! A wheelbarrow uses levers and a wheel and axle.

You push the button and the wall slides away. Around the corner, there's a deep canyon! It's too wide to jump across, so you'll need to build a bridge.

Next to the canyon, there's some building blocks and two long, flat planks. This is easy! You'll use them as a bridge. But when you try, neither piece is long enough.

Suddenly, a voice startles you. It's coming from the wall!

For a clue, answer this question. What kind of bridge do you need to build? A suspension bridge or cantilever?

What do you say?

A SUSPENSION BRIDGE
GO TO PAGE 12

A CANTILEVER
TURN TO PAGE 38

Correct! An automaton is a machine, such as a robot. Once it has been set in motion, it can work without a human controlling it.

The knight steps out of your way. In front of you is a locked door, a note, and a clockwork toy with a key in its hand. Next to the toy is a clock, a spring, and a battery.

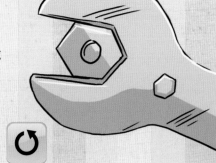

Fix the toy to pass.

Which part is needed to drive a clockwork toy?

CLOCK
HEAD TO PAGE 5

SPRING
GO TO PAGE 19

BATTERY
TURN TO PAGE 26

 No! Archaeopteryx was a flying creature from the time of the dinosaurs.

GO BACK TO PAGE 12
AND **TRY A BIT HARDER**

Right on! A little flexing keeps the wheels in contact with the track.

The judge smiles and moves on to the next workstation. You attach the wheels firmly. The last thing you want is for your wheels to fall off!

Which way do you turn the wrench to tighten each nut?

CLOCKWISE
GO TO PAGE 9

**COUNTER-
CLOCKWISE**
GO TO PAGE 23

YES! A pulley is a simple machine that uses wheels and ropes to raise or lower a load.

A cheer erupts as the judge hands you the trophy and a check for the prize money. Spanner Spike starts to cry. The crowd parts as Mr. Jollypops walks through. You hand him the check.

You have saved Toy Towers. As a thank you, I'd like to make you part-owner of the factory. Congratulations!

 Yes, each of the colored cubes rotates around an axle, in the same way as a wheel turns on a car.

Correct!
Let's see what else you know. What makes this caterpillar wriggle?

He turns a handle and a wooden caterpillar on his desk begins to wriggle.

CLOCKWORK GEARS
HEAD OVER TO PAGE 28

ROTATING CAMS
TURN TO PAGE 17

Awesome! If you mount the camera on the end of the spring, when the box is opened, it'll shoot out to snap the culprit in the act—just like a jack-in-the-box.

YOU SET THE TRAP AND GO TO PAGE 5

 No! Turning the steering wheel sharply when you're traveling at high speeds will make you lose control. You'll crash!

GO BACK TO PAGE 10
AND **TRY AGAIN**

 Oh dear! You've spelled out mechanics, which relates to the science of machinery.

HAVE ANOTHER
TRY ON PAGE 29

No, pneumatic machines use pressurized air to make things move.

HAVE ANOTHER TRY ON PAGE 12

Fantastic! A lever multiplies your muscle power as you pull it.

Your car is finally finished! An announcement tells you what to do next.

"The race will begin at 9 a.m. tomorrow. Put your cars into the storage boxes and go home. If anyone tries to make modifications, they will be disqualified."

When you roll your car toward the storage box, one of the wheels falls off! The nut is loose—but you're sure you tightened them all. . . . First, you're offered oil and now this. Someone must be trying to sabotage your car!

SMALL FORCE ON LEVER →

EXTRA FORCE ON BRAKE CABLE ←

What security device could you add to catch any culprits in the act?

A BUTTON THAT DELIVERS AN ELECTRIC SHOCK. GO TO PAGE 21

A CAMERA SO YOU HAVE PHOTOGRAPHIC EVIDENCE. TURN TO PAGE 13

SOME **SUPERGLUE** SO THE CULPRIT GETS STUCK. HEAD TO PAGE 27

Incorrect! A wedge is made of two inclined planes. It helps you to push things apart.

TRY AGAIN
ON PAGE 20

 Zero points! Magnetism is a force, but it doesn't make roller coasters move.

HEAD TO PAGE 41
TO **TRY AGAIN**

 No, a high gear is good for speeding along a flat area. You have to push hard on the pedals to drive the wheels around, but the wheels turn very fast. That's not going to work going uphill!

TRY AGAIN
ON PAGE 24

 Yes, a cantilever is a long beam that is fixed at one end. With a cantilever bridge, the beams project from either side to meet in the middle.

A message appears on the wall.

TO BUILD A CANTILEVER BRIDGE, ADD WEIGHTS.

Of course! You start looking for something really heavy, when you notice that some of the building blocks are marked with weight measurements.

How do you build your bridge?

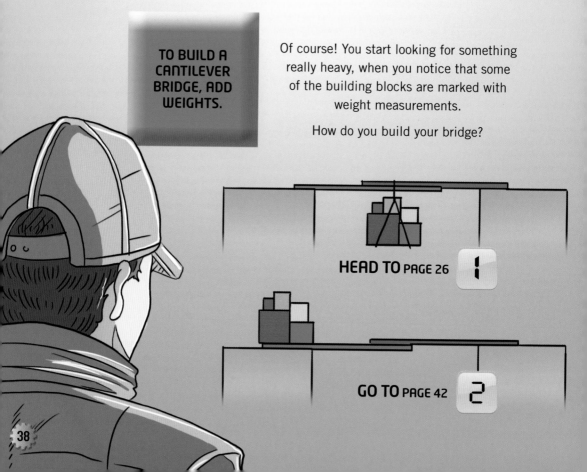

HEAD TO PAGE 26

GO TO PAGE 42

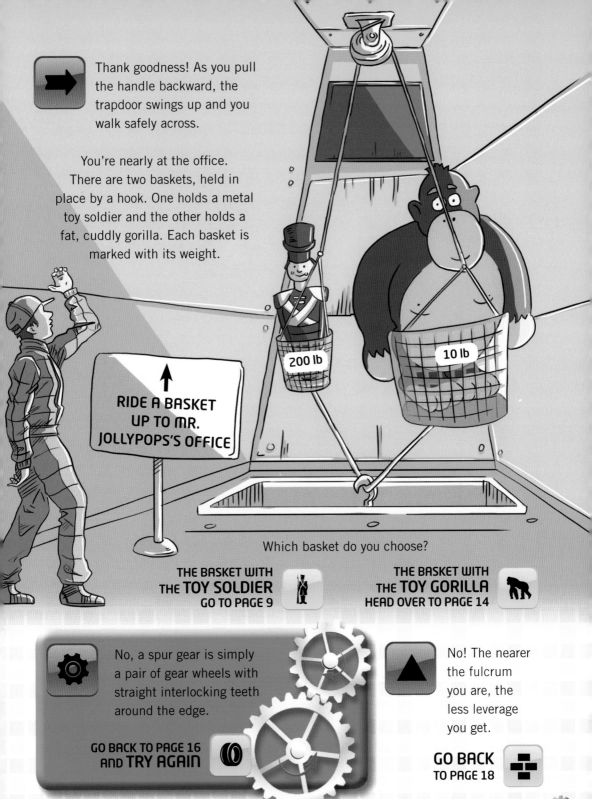

Thank goodness! As you pull the handle backward, the trapdoor swings up and you walk safely across.

You're nearly at the office. There are two baskets, held in place by a hook. One holds a metal toy soldier and the other holds a fat, cuddly gorilla. Each basket is marked with its weight.

200 lb

10 lb

↑
RIDE A BASKET
UP TO MR.
JOLLYPOPS'S OFFICE

Which basket do you choose?

THE BASKET WITH
THE **TOY SOLDIER**
GO TO PAGE 9

THE BASKET WITH
THE **TOY GORILLA**
HEAD OVER TO PAGE 14

No, a spur gear is simply a pair of gear wheels with straight interlocking teeth around the edge.

GO BACK TO PAGE 16
AND **TRY AGAIN**

No! The nearer the fulcrum you are, the less leverage you get.

GO BACK
TO PAGE 18

AB Great! As you turn the knob (which acts like a wheel), the rod (which acts like an axle) turns, which works the mechanism inside the door. Turning the axle without a knob would be much more difficult.

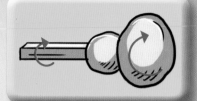

You take a deep breath and stride through the open door. . .

You walk into a maze made of brightly colored Rubik's Cubes. The walls are high and there seems to be no way through.

A question appears before you.

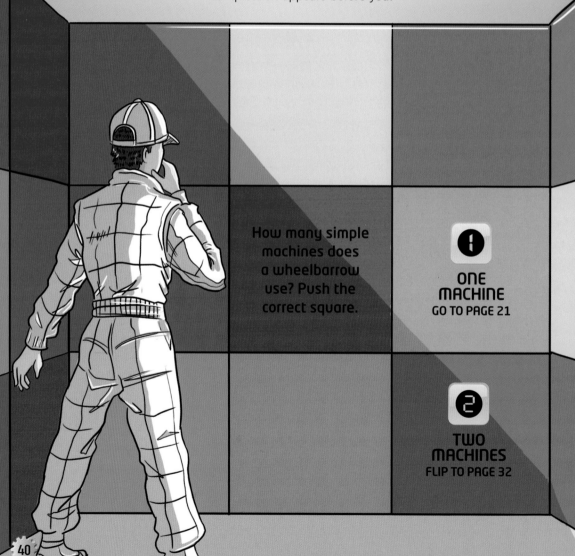

How many simple machines does a wheelbarrow use? Push the correct square.

❶

ONE MACHINE
GO TO PAGE 21

❷

TWO MACHINES
FLIP TO PAGE 32

Yes, mechanical advantage measures how much easier a machine makes a job.

You pull the lever and hurtle down the slope. You're surely going to crash and there are no brakes! Finally the carriage starts to slow down next to a door.

You climb out and try to open the door. It's stuck! A small panel above the handle lights up.

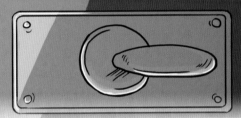

SECURITY CODE

What is the force that helped to give the roller coaster its speed?

ELECTRICITY
TURN TO PAGE 13

MAGNETISM
FLIP TO PAGE 38

GRAVITY
GO TO PAGE 6

 Oh no! That's just about the worst shape you could choose. The air will bash into the flat front of the car and really slow you down.

GO BACK TO PAGE 31 AND TRY AGAIN

 Yes, a low gear is just right for climbing a hill. You pedal fast, which turns the wheels slowly but with a lot of force. You're up the bank and back into the race in no time.

You pedal hard and reach the finish line. The other competitors are already out of their cars, so you came last.

HEAD TO THE PITS
ON PAGE 16

The lever, wheel and axle, and screw are simple machines, but the crank, plough, and hammer are not.

 GO BACK TO PAGE 23 AND TRY AGAIN

 Wrong! Weight is a force (the force of gravity), and Newtons are the correct measure of force. Only mass should be measured in pounds.

GO BACK TO PAGE 5

2 Yes, the weights act as a balance to stop the planks tipping into the canyon. You walk along the first plank and place the second plank down, completing the bridge.

As you edge across the second plank, you see Spanner Spike behind you—and he's removing the weights! You step to safety as the planks drop into the canyon. Spike yells out in dismay as he realizes he's stuck on the other side.

In front of you are two doorways with a question above them.

What is the weight moved by a machine called?

EFFORT
GO THROUGH THE RIGHT-HAND DOORWAY TO PAGE 9

LOAD
GO THROUGH THE LEFT-HAND DOORWAY TO PAGE 20

42

Yes, Archimedes was one of the greatest scientists ever. He proved the basic theory of the machine—that a small effort can move a large load if it is spread out over a distance.

 "Second question: Is an ax a machine?"

DEFINITELY. TURN TO PAGE 23 **OF COURSE NOT! GO TO PAGE 8**

 Try again! A spring isn't used to push an elevator to the top.

TURN BACK TO PAGE 21

The judges are waiting for you and Spike.

Good job, Spanner Spike. You've nearly beaten the others in this final task to be crowned Young Toymaker of the Year. But we have a final question for you. What simple machine is the basis of all cranes?

Spanner Spike looks dumbstruck. He doesn't know the answer!

Spanner Spike, if you cannot answer such a simple question, how did you get this far? I hope you didn't cheat!

Spanner Spike turns a bright shade of red.

The judge turns to you.

If you can answer, you will win the prize. What simple machine is the basis of all cranes?

SCREW GO TO PAGE 26

PULLEY FLIP TO PAGE 34

GL☼SSARY

Apprentice

Someone who works for an employer, usually for a short period of time, to learn a skill or job.

Automaton

A machine that moves by itself, especially one that mimics a living creature, such as a person or an animal.

Cam

A wheel with one part raised to push against a rod each time the wheel turns. It changes this circular movement into forward and backward movements.

Clockwork

A mechanism driven by a wound-up spring, like an old-fashioned clock.

Crane

A tall machine with a long arm and a pulley system. It is used to lift and move heavy objects, such as bricks on a building site.

Effort

The force used to make a machine work.

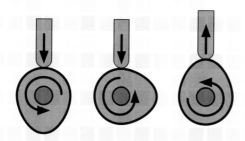

In a cam, the wheel is often egg-shaped to push the rod upward.

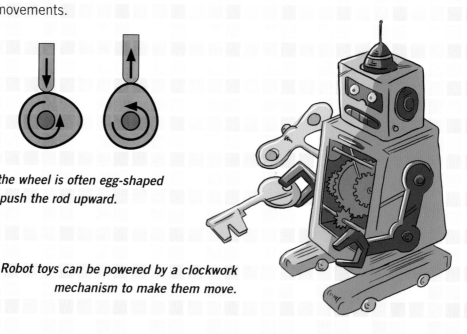

Robot toys can be powered by a clockwork mechanism to make them move.

Force

The amount of strength or power with which something moves.

Friction

A force that stops one surface from sliding easily over another surface. This force slows down moving objects. For example, if you try to slide a book across a table, the friction between the book and the table quickly slows and stops the book.

Fulcrum

The point or pivot at which a lever swivels or hinges, or is supported to lift something.

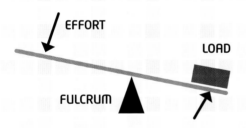

A see-saw has a fulcrum in the middle. The load and effort are the people sitting at each end.

Gear

A toothed wheel that interlocks with another gear. When one wheel turns, it turns the other gear. If one wheel has more teeth than the other, it will turn more slowly, but with more force. For example, cars use gears to get extra force to turn the wheels when climbing hills.

Spur gears are the most common type of gear. They have straight teeth.

Gravity

The force that pulls all things together, and makes things fall to the ground. Gravity is what holds you on the ground.

Handicap weight

Extra weight put on a racer to ensure all the racers start at the same weight.

Hydraulic

When something is powered by the pressure of fluid moving through tubes.

Invent

To think of a new idea for something, such as creating a new machine.

Lever

A simple machine that is a rigid bar that pivots at a point called a fulcrum. It multiplies your effort so you can move something heavy.

Load

The weight or pressure moved by a machine.

Machine

A man-made device with moving parts that performs a particular task.

Magnetism

The force between magnetic materials such as iron and nickel. It can either pull them together or push them apart.

Mechanical advantage

The extra strength given by a machine. It is a measure of how much easier a machine makes a job.

Mechanism

The part of a machine, or a set of parts, that does a particular job.

Momentum

The tendency of an object to keep going once it has started moving. The heavier it is and the faster it is traveling, the more momentum it has.

Newton

The unit used to measure force.

Pedal

A lever driven by your foot. A bicycle has two pedals that are pushed by the rider's feet to make the bicycle move forward.

A bicycle pedal is a special type of lever called a crank

Piston

A cylinder that slides up and down inside another. In an engine, pistons are pushed by expanding gases to give the force to drive a car.

Pneumatic

When something is powered by the pressure of air or gases moving through tubes.

Pulley

A simple machine made of a rope or chain wrapped around a wheel. The rope or chain is pulled to lift heavy things easily.

Rack and pinion

A mechanism that has a toothed wheel (the pinion) rolling along a toothed bar (the rack) so that the rack moves from side to side as the wheel turns. A rack and pinion gear system is used by trains to travel up steep hills.

Simple machine

A simple machine is a device with just one part that makes a task quicker or need less effort. The six simple machines are the lever, inclined plane (ramp), wedge, pulley, screw, and wheel and axle.

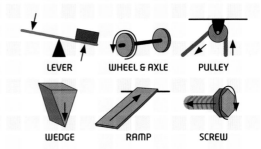

LEVER   WHEEL & AXLE   PULLEY

WEDGE   RAMP   SCREW

There are six simple machines. Sometimes they are used together. A wheelbarrow uses the lever and wheel and axle.

Spokes

Thin rods that connect the center of a wheel to its rim. Bicycle wheels have thin, metal spokes.

Spokes are arranged in a crisscross pattern for maximum strength.

Taking it further

The Rubik's Quest series is designed to motivate children to develop their Science, Technology, Engineering, and Mathematics (STEM) skills. They will learn how to apply their know-how to the world through engaging adventure stories involving the Rubik's Cube, a mind-bending puzzle used throughout the world by people of all ages. For each book, readers must solve a series of problems to make progress toward the exciting conclusion.

The books do not follow a conventional pattern. The reader is directed to jump forward and back through the book according to the answers he or she gives to the problems. If the answers are correct, the reader progresses to the next part of the story; if they are incorrect the reason is explained, before the reader is directed back to try the problem again. Additional support may be found in the glossary at the back of the book.

To support your child's development you can:

- Read the book with your child.

- Solve the initial problems and discover how the book works.

- Continue reading with your child until he or she is using the book confidently, following the **"GO TO"** instructions to find the next puzzle or explanation.

- Encourage your child to read on alone. Ask "What's happening now?" Prompt your child to tell you how the story develops and what problems they have solved.

- Discuss machines in everyday contexts, such as opening a door; using a screwdriver or a hammer; climbing the stairs; turning faucets; and using gears, brakes, and pedals on a bicycle.

- Have fun playing on a see-saw, shifting your weights along the seat to alter the balance.

- See how many places you can spot simple machines.

- Try lifting different weights together, with your arm straight or bent. Which is easier? Help your child to explain and understand the result.

- Use simple machines to perform simple tasks, such as getting the lid off a paint can, or lifting a heavy weight.

- Ask your child to invent and build simple machines using a construction kit such as Lego.

- Most of all, make learning fun!